EASY GUITAR ANTHOLOGY

SANTANA

20 GREATEST HITS

Arranged by Hemme Luttjeboer

Project Managers: Aaron Stang & Colgan Bryan
Project Coordinator: Karl Bork
Art Design: Debbie Johns
Engraver: Musical/Arts Consultants Inc.
Technical Editor: Jack Allen

CD Artwork:

Supernatural
© 1999 Arista Inc.

Zebop!
© 1981 CBS Inc.

Moonflower
© 1977 CBS Inc.

Viva Santana!
© 1988 CBS Inc.

Inner Secrets
© 1978 CBS Inc.

Abraxas
© 1970 CBS Inc.

Blues for Salvador
© 1987 CBS Inc.

Santana
© 1969 CBS Inc.

© 2001 WARNER BROS. PUBLICATIONS
All Rights Reserved

Any duplication, adaptation or arrangement of the compositions
contained in this collection requires the written consent of the Publisher.
No part of this book may be photocopied or reproduced in any way without permission.
Unauthorized uses are an infringement of the U.S. Copyright Act and are punishable by law.

MW00564881

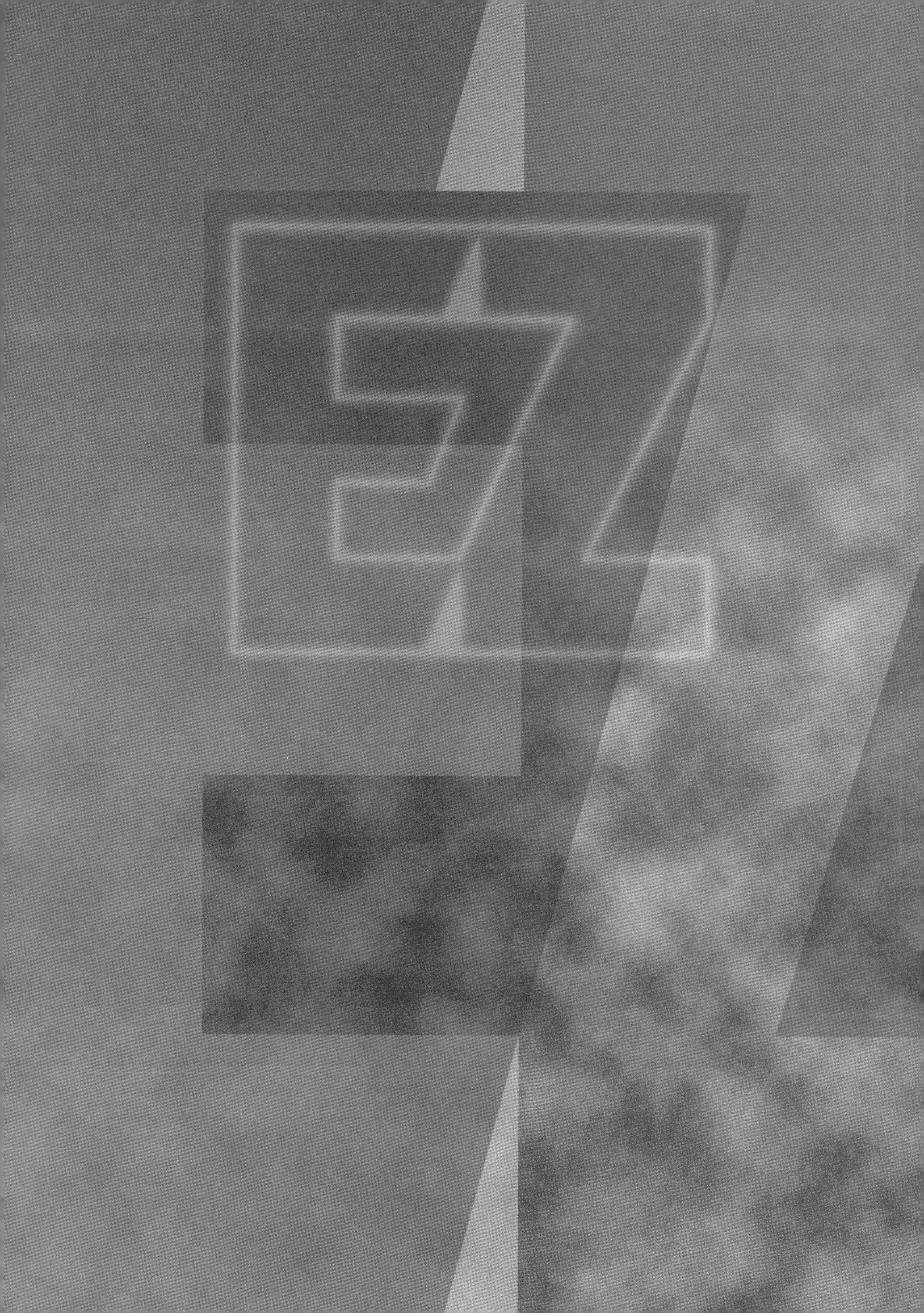

CONTENTS

BELLA

Words and Music by
CARLOS SANTANA, CHESTER THOMPSON
and STERLING CREW

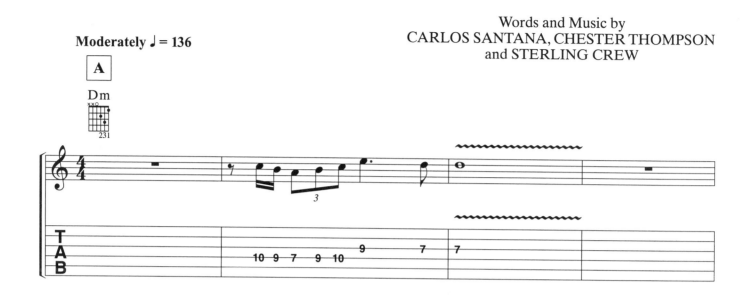

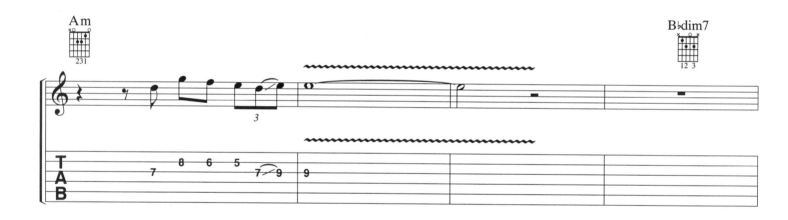

Bella - 6 - 1
PGM0027

© 1987 LIGHT MUSIC (BMI) and URMILA MUSIC (ASCAP)
All Rights Reserved

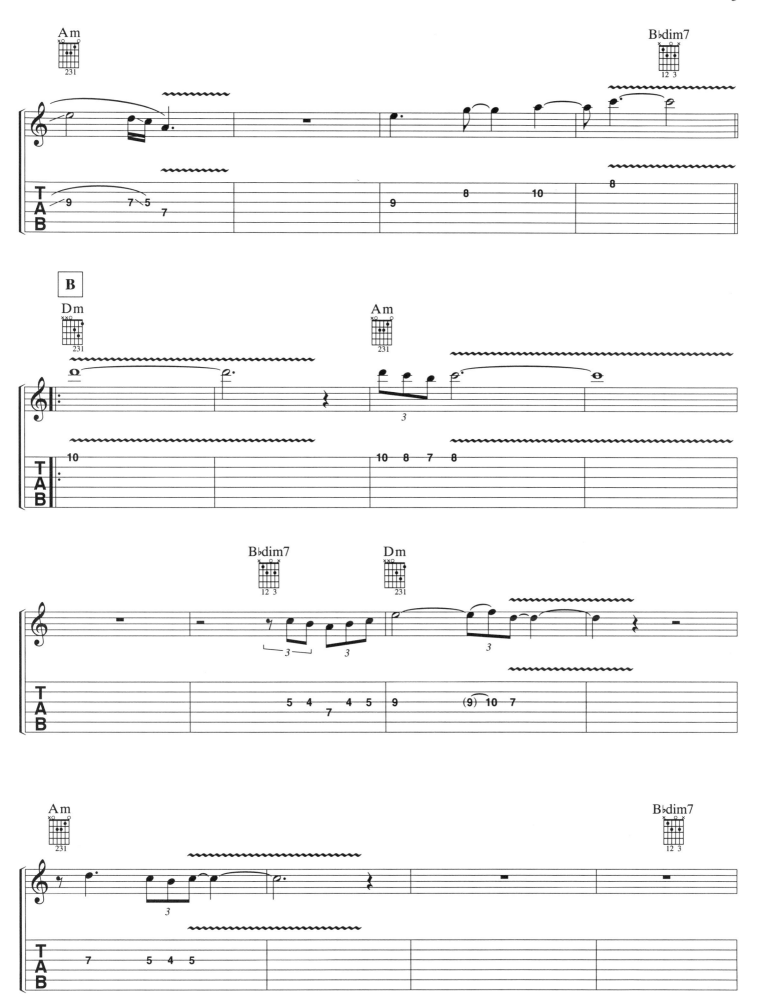

6

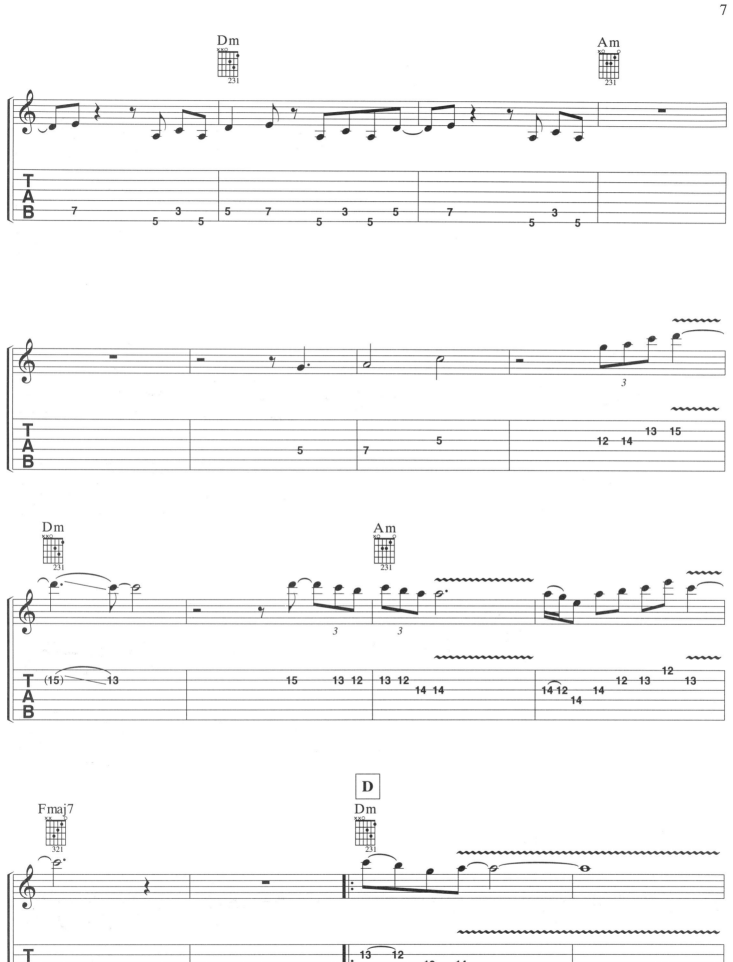

Bella - 6 - 5
PGM0027

Outro:

Repeat and fade

BLACK MAGIC WOMAN/GYPSY QUEEN

Words and Music by
PETER GREEN

© Copyright 1968 by King Publishing Co., Ltd., London, England
Copyright Renewed
© Copyright 1970 by King Publishing Co., Ltd., London, England
Copyright Renewed
This Arrangement © Copyright 2001 by Murbo Music Publishing Inc.
World-wide Rights Assigned to Bourne Music Ltd.
All Rights for the U.S.A. and Canada Controlled by Murbo Music Publishing Inc.
All Rights Reserved   Used by Permission

Black Mag - ic Wom - an,   got me so blind I can't___ see   that she's a
back on me, ba - by,   stop mess - in' 'round with your___ tricks.   Don't turn your

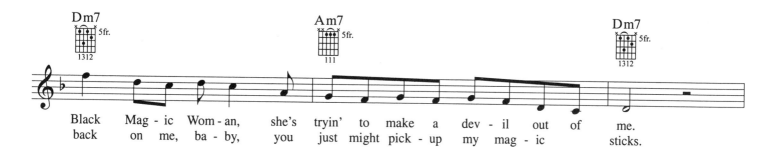

Black Mag - ic Wom - an, she's tryin' to make a dev - il out of me.
back on me, ba - by,   you just might pick - up my mag - ic sticks.

1.2.3.

2. I   got   a   Black   Mag - ic
3. Don't turn your back on me, ba -
4. You got your spell on me, ba -

4. *Outro:*

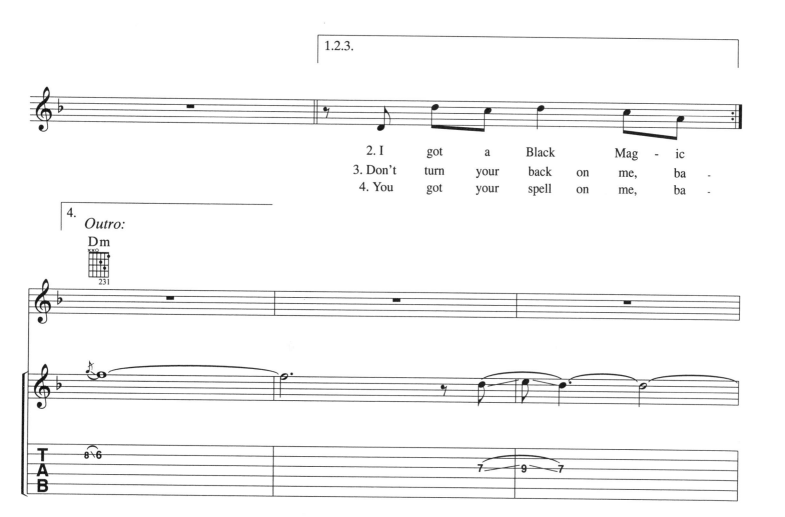

GYPSY QUEEN

Music by
GABOR SZABO

Moderately fast ♩ = 144
N.C.

D

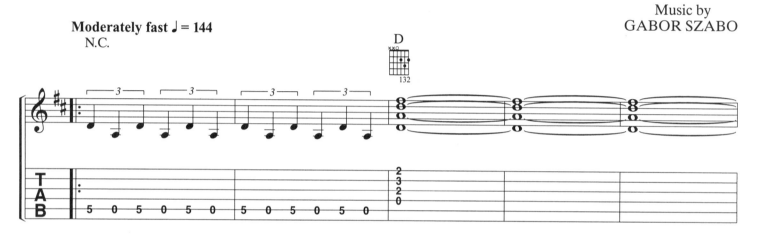

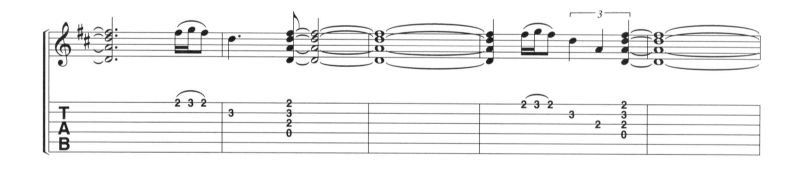

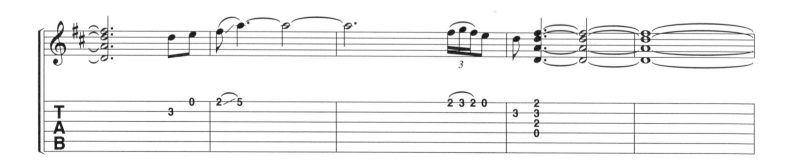

Black Magic Woman/Gypsy Queen - 4 - 3
PGM0027

© 1966 (Renewed 1994) GABOR & CARDIGAN MUSIC (BMI)
All Rights Reserved   Used by Permission

Verse 4:
You got your spell on me, baby,
You got your spell on me, baby,
Turnin' my heart into stone.
I need you so bad, magic woman,
I can't leave you alone.
(To Outro:)

Black Magic Woman/Gypsy Queen - 4 - 4
PGM0027

EUROPA
(Earth's Cry Heaven's Smile)

Music by
CARLOS SANTANA and TOM COSTER

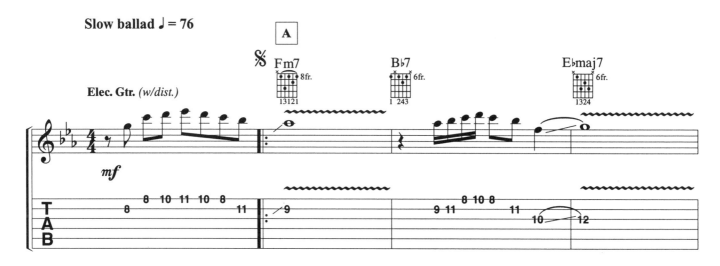

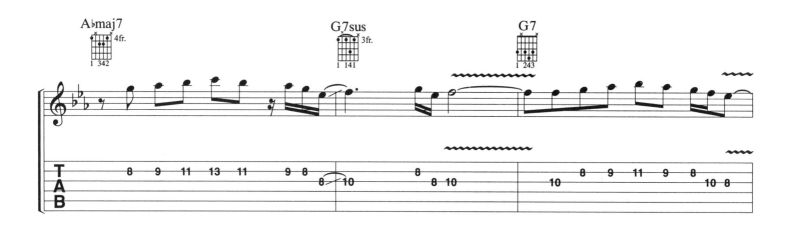

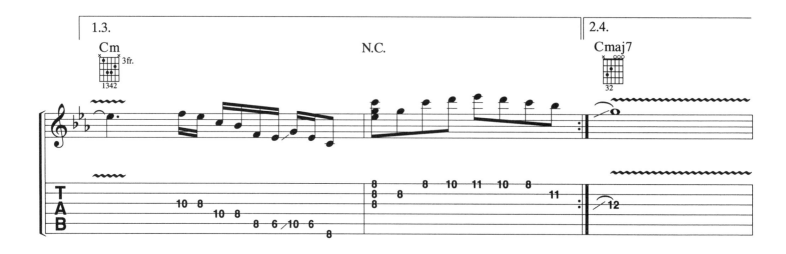

Europa - 2 - 1
PGM0027

© 1976 LIGHT MUSIC (BMI)
All Rights Reserved

EVERYBODY'S EVERYTHING

Words and Music by
CARLOS SANTANA, TYRONE MOSS
and MILTON BROWN

Moderate rock ♩ = 136

Verse 1:

E7

Seems like ev-'ry-bod-y's wait-in' for a new change to come a-

round.

(Come a-round,__ come a-round,__ come a-round.__)

Wait-in' for the day when the

E7

king and queens of soul sing-in' 'round.__

(Sing-in' 'round,__ sing-in' 'round,__ sing-in' 'round.__)

B7   A7   E5   D5   D♯5 E5   B7(♯9)

(1.) Sing - in' 'round, sing-in' 'round__ for ev-'ry-one.   You can }
  2. Dig   this sound it's been a-round__ and 'round and 'round. Could you }

Chorus:

E7

un-der-stand__ ev-'ry-thing's to share.   Let your spir-it dance,__ broth-ers,

Everybody's Everything - 3 - 1
PGM0027

© 1971 PETRA MUSIC and DANDELION MUSIC (BMI)
All Rights Reserved

ev - 'ry - where.___ Let your___ head be free,___ turn the wis-dom key. Find it___

B7

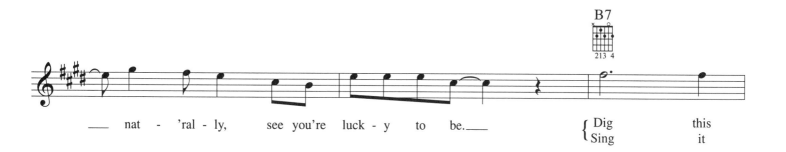

___ nat - 'ral - ly, see you're luck - y to be.___ { Dig this
Sing it

A7

To Coda

E5 D5 D#5 E5 B7(#9)

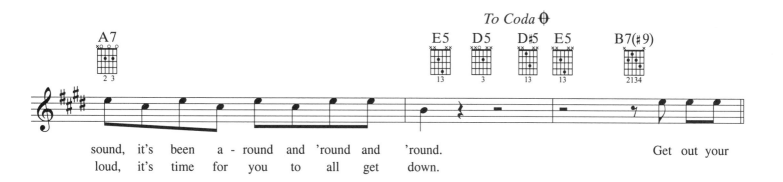

sound, it's been a - round and 'round and 'round. Get out your
loud, it's time for you to all get down.

Verse 2:

E7

cold feet, ba - by. Some - thin' on your back, let it down.
(Let it down,___ let it down,___

A7

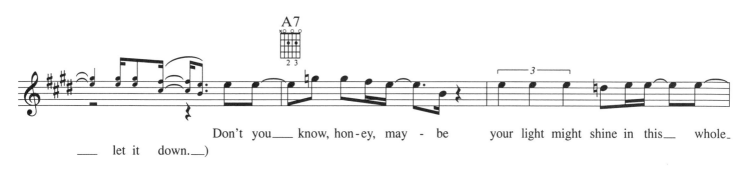

Don't you___ know, hon-ey, may - be your light might shine in this___ whole___
___ let it down.___)

18

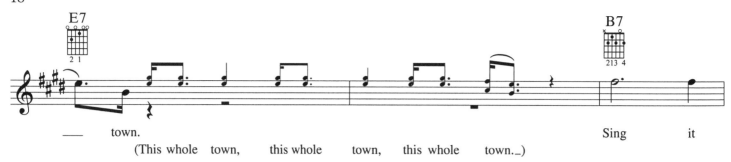

—— town.

(This whole town, this whole town, this whole town.—)

Sing it

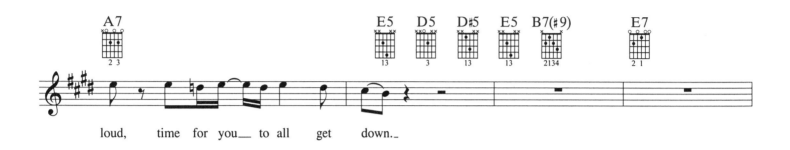

loud, time for you—— to all get down.—

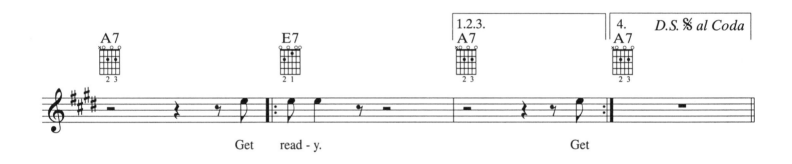

Get read - y.

Get

Guitar Solo: *Play 12 times*

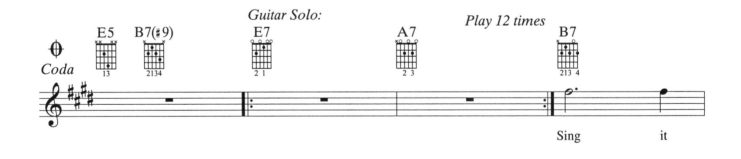

Sing it

Guitar Solo: *Repeat and fade*

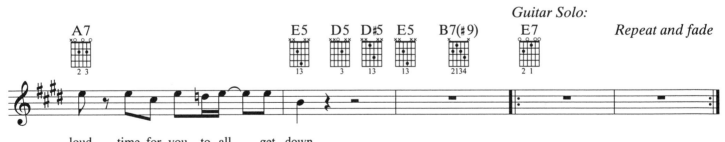

loud, time for you to all—— get down.

I'LL BE WAITING

Words and Music by
CARLOS SANTANA

Moderately ♩ = 119

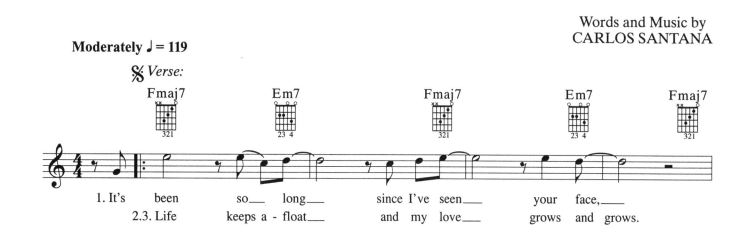

1. It's been so long since I've seen your face,
2.3. Life keeps a-float and my love grows and grows.

yet I know soon I'll have your em-brace. I'll be wait-
You are the light, you are the light and the way. I'll be wait-

To Coda ⊕

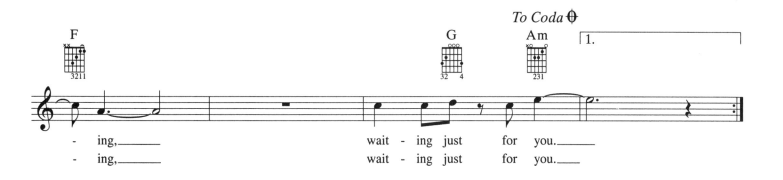

- ing, wait-ing just for you.
- ing, wait-ing just for you.

Bridge:

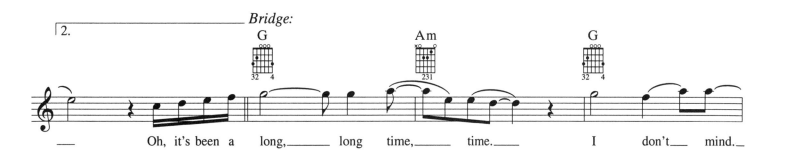

Oh, it's been a long, long time, time. I don't mind.

I'll Be Waiting - 3 - 1
PGM0027

© 1977 LIGHT MUSIC (BMI)
All Rights Reserved

21

Interlude:

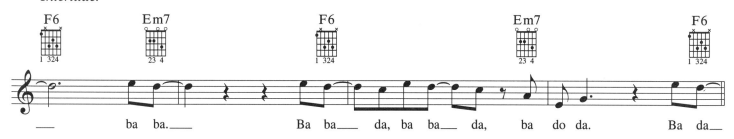

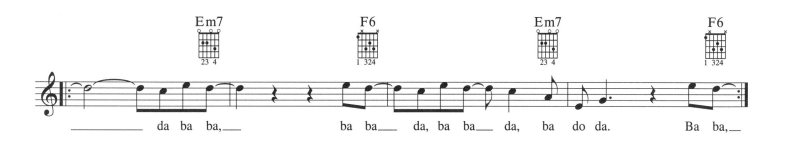

Guitar Solo: *Repeat as needed*

Outro: *Repeat and fade*

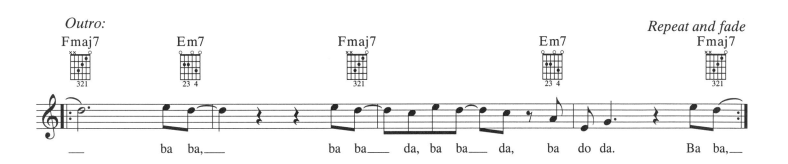

EVIL WAYS

Words and Music by
CLARENCE HENRY

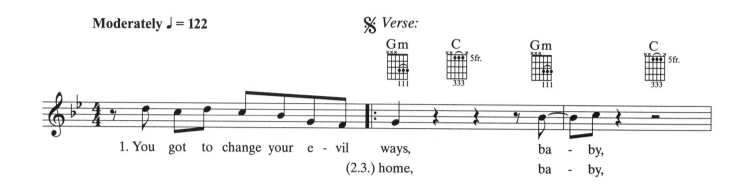

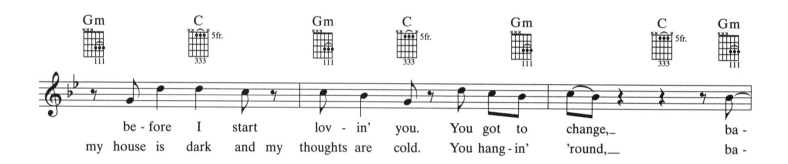

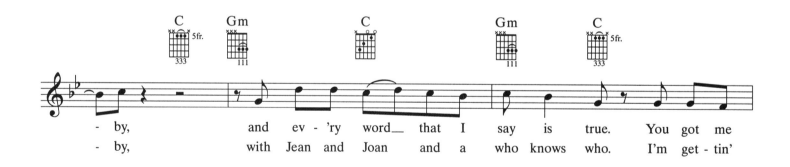

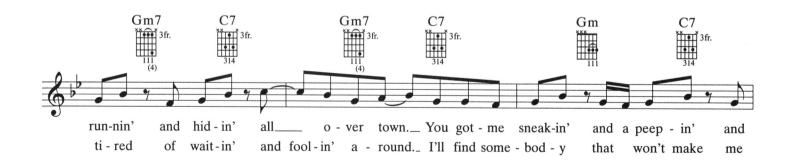

© 1967 Richcar Music (Renewed)
All Rights Administered by Universal - Songs of PolyGram International, Inc.
All Rights Reserved

JINGO
(Ji-Go-Lo-Ba)

Words and Music by
MICHAEL OLANTUNJI

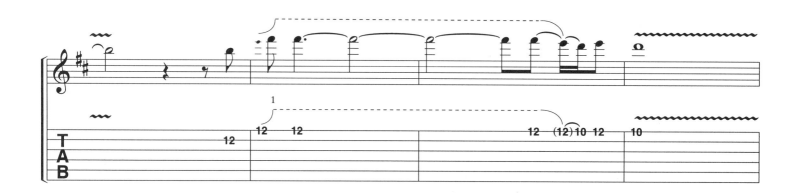

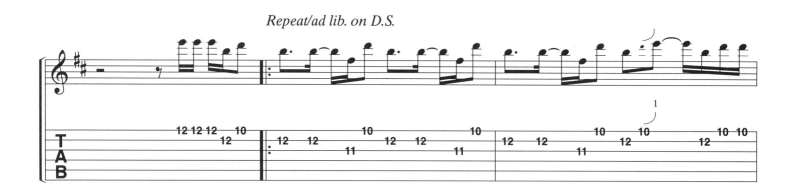

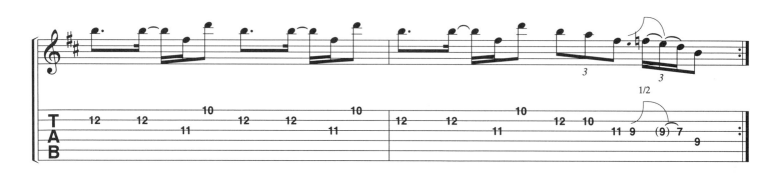

Jingo - 2 - 1
PGM0027

© 1961 (Renewed 1989) EMI Blackwood Music, Inc.
All Rights Reserved   Used by Permission

25

Interlude: *Chorus:*

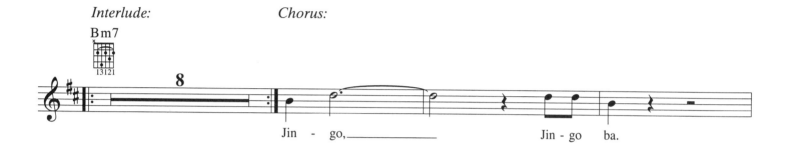

Jin - go,_____ Jin - go ba.

Jin - go,_____ Jin - go ba. Jin - go

Fine
Repeat till fade on D.S.

ba, ba, lo, ba, ba, lo, ba, ba, lo, ba. Lo, ba, ba, lo, ba, ba, lo, ba, ba, lo, ba.

D.S. % al Fine
Percussion/Organ solos:
Repeat till cue

Jin - go,_____ Jin - go ba.

LOVE OF MY LIFE

Words and Music by
CARLOS SANTANA and DAVE MATTHEWS

Moderately ♩ = 96
Verse 1:

Where you are, that's where I wan-na be.___ And through your eyes,_____ all

the things I wan-na see. And in the night, you are my dream, you're ev-'ry-thing to___

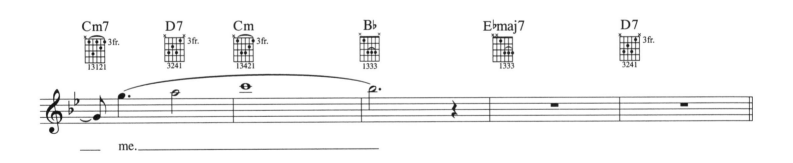

___ me.___

Chorus 1:

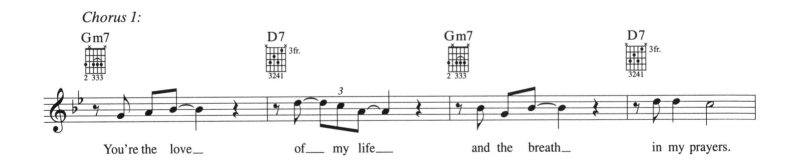

You're the love___ of___ my life___ and the breath___ in my prayers.

Love of My Life - 3 - 1
PGM0027

© 1999 STELLABELLA MUSIC (BMI) and COLDEN GREY LTD. (ASCAP)
All Rights Reserved

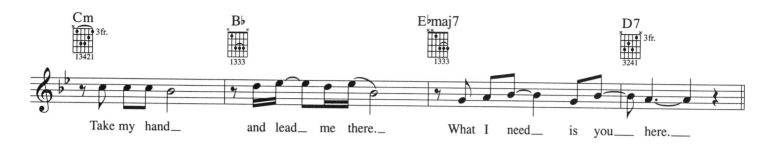

Take my hand__ and lead__ me there.__ What I need__ is you__ here.__

Verse 2:

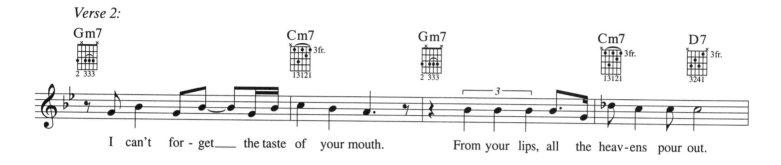

I can't for - get__ the taste of your mouth. From your lips, all the heav-ens pour out.

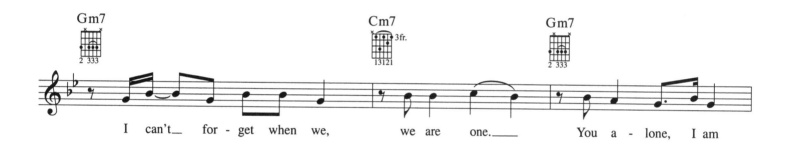

I can't__ for - get when we, we are one.__ You a - lone, I am

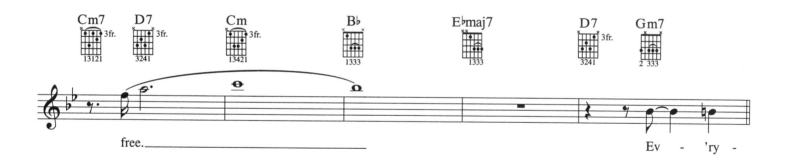

free._____

Ev - 'ry -

Chorus 2:

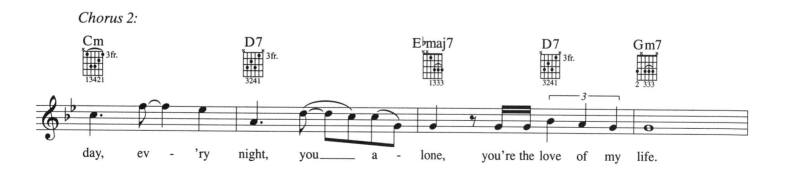

day, ev - 'ry night, you__ a - lone, you're the love of my life.

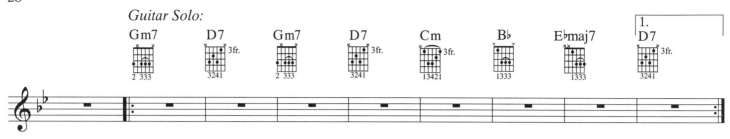

Guitar Solo:

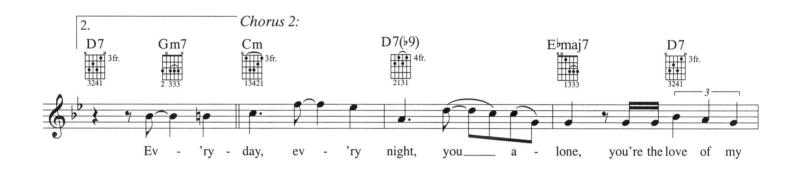

Ev - 'ry-day, ev-'ry night, you____ a - lone, you're the love of my

life. We go danc-ing in the moon - light____ with the star-light in your

eyes.____ We go danc-ing 'til____ the sun - rise.____ You and me, we're gon-na

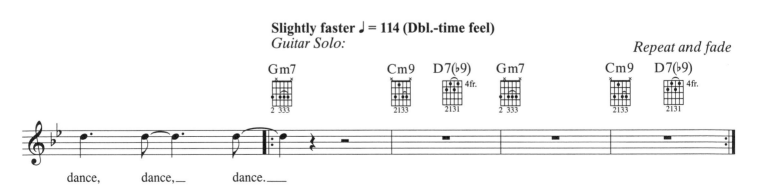

dance, dance,____ dance.____

MARIA MARIA

Words and Music by
WYCLEF JEAN, JERRY DUPLESSIS,
CARLOS SANTANA, KARL PERAZZO and RAUL REKOW

Moderately ♩ = 96

𝄉 *Chorus:*

Oh, Ma-ri-a, Ma-ri-a._____ She re-minds_ me of a west-side sto-ry_____

grow-ing up in Span-ish Har-lem._____ She's liv-ing the life just like_ a mov-ie star. Oh,_

___ Ma-ri-a, Ma-ri-a,_____ she fell in love_ in east L. A.,_____

To Coda ⊕

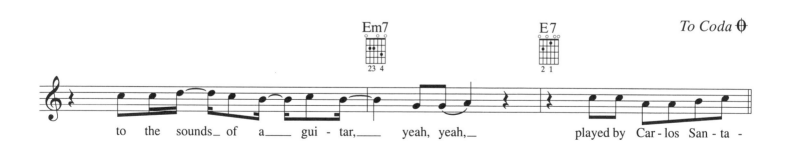

to the sounds_ of a gui-tar,_____ yeah, yeah,_ played by Car-los San-ta-

Maria Maria - 5 - 1
PGM0027

© 1999 SONY/ATV TUNES LLC, HUSS ZWINGLI PUBLISHING INC. (ASCAP),
TEBASS MUSIC, EMI BLACKWOOD MUSIC INC. and STELLABELLA MUSIC (BMI)
All Rights Reserved

30

Interlude:
Am

na.

Elec. Gtr. *(w/dist.)*

mf

Verse 1:

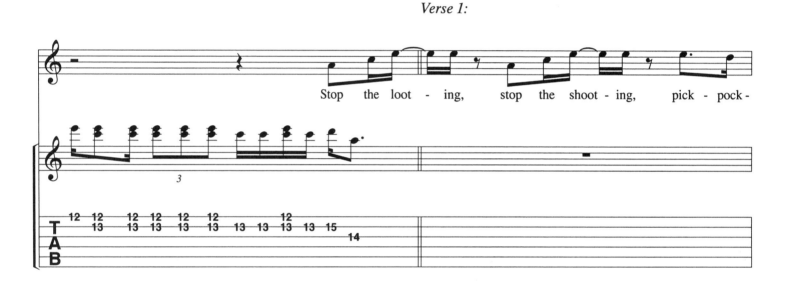

Stop the loot - ing, stop the shoot - ing, pick - pock -

G   F   G   E/G#

ing on the cor-ner. See as the rich is get-ting rich-er, the poor is get-ting poor-er. Se mi-ra Ma-ri-

Am   G   F

a on the cor-ner think-ing of ways to make it bet-ter. In my mail-box there's an e-vic-tion let-ter.

Maria Maria - 5 - 2
PGM0027

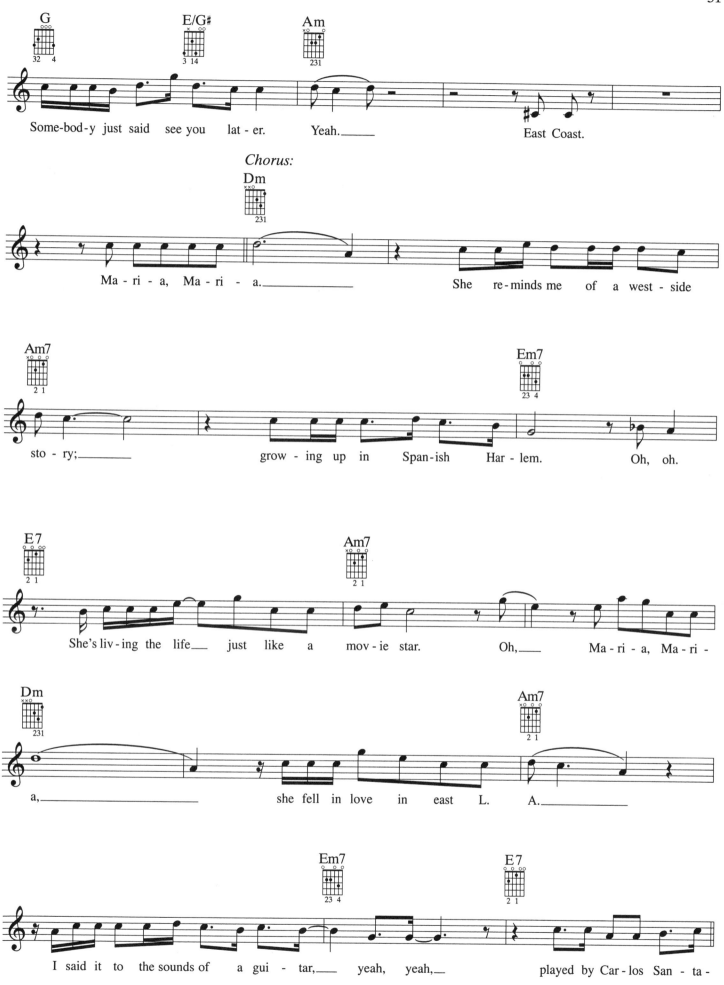

Interlude:

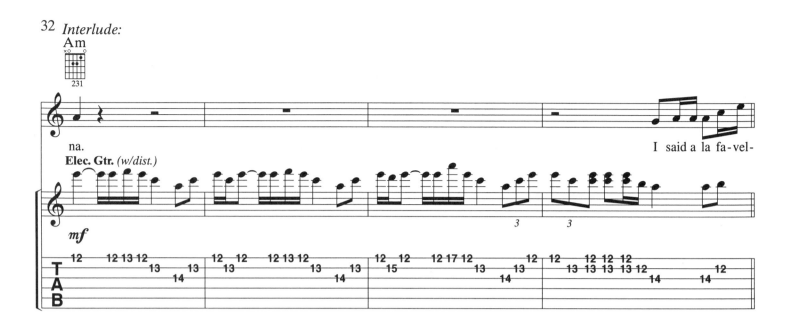

na.

Elec. Gtr. *(w/dist.)*

mf

I said a la fa-vel-

Verse 2:

la los co-lo-res. The streets are get-ting hot-ter. There is no wa-ter to put out the fi-re. Mi can-

to la es-per-ran-za. Se mi-ra Ma-ri-a on the cor-ner, think-ing of ways to make it bet-ter. Then I looked

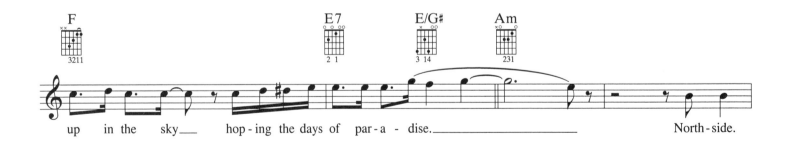

up in the sky___ hop-ing the days of par-a-dise.___ North-side.

South-side. World-wide. O-pen up your eyes.

Verse 3:

Ma - ri - a, you know you're my lov - er._____ When the wind blows, I can

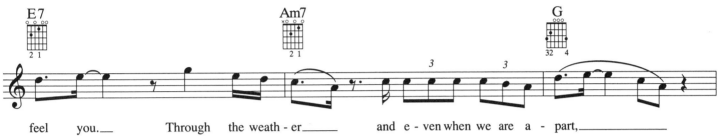

feel you.__ Through the weath - er_____ and e - ven when we are a - part,_____

D.S. % al Coda

it still feels__ like we're to - geth - er. Ma - ri -

Coda

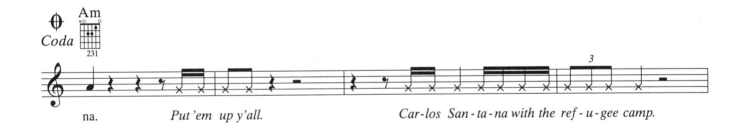

na. *Put 'em up y'all.* *Car-los San-ta-na with the ref-u-gee camp.*

Wy-clef, *Jer-ry Won-der,* *Mis-ter San-ta-na,* *G and B.*

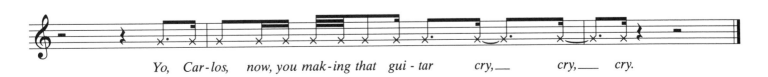

Yo, Car-los, now, you mak-ing that gui-tar cry,__ cry,__ cry.

Maria Maria - 5 - 5
PGM0027

OPEN INVITATION

Words and Music by
CARLOS SANTANA, GREG WALKER, DAVID MARGEN,
DENNIS LAMBERT and BRIAN POTTER

Moderately ♩ = 94

Verse:

1. You be you   and let me be me.___   No strings at - tached,___   e - like
2. Let's make love,   the feel-ing is right.___   Just pass - in' by,___   like
3. *Guitar solo*

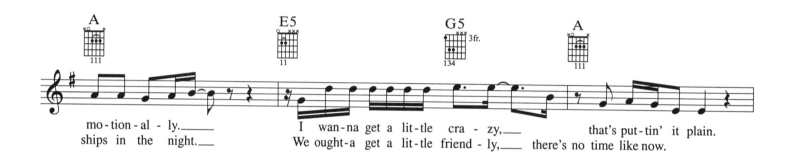

mo - tion - al - ly.___   I wan-na get a lit-tle cra - zy,___   that's put-tin' it plain.
ships in the night.___   We ought-a get a lit-tle friend - ly,___   there's no time like now.

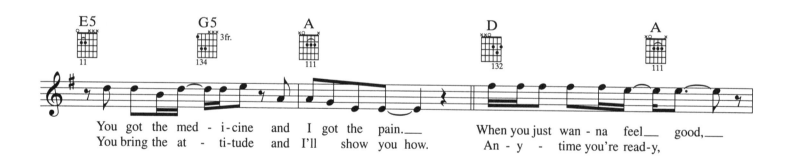

You got the med - i - cine and I got the pain.___   When you just wan - na feel__ good,___
You bring the at - ti-tude and I'll show you how.   An - y - time you're read-y,

like the doc - tor said,___   one good dose of lov - in'   is gon-na   straight-en out___   your head..
an - y - time__ at all,___   just come on o - ver,   you   don't e - ven have to call.___

Open Invitation - 3 - 1
PGM0027

© 1978 LIGHT MUSIC (BMI) and LAMBERT & POTTER MUSIC (BMI)
All Rights Reserved

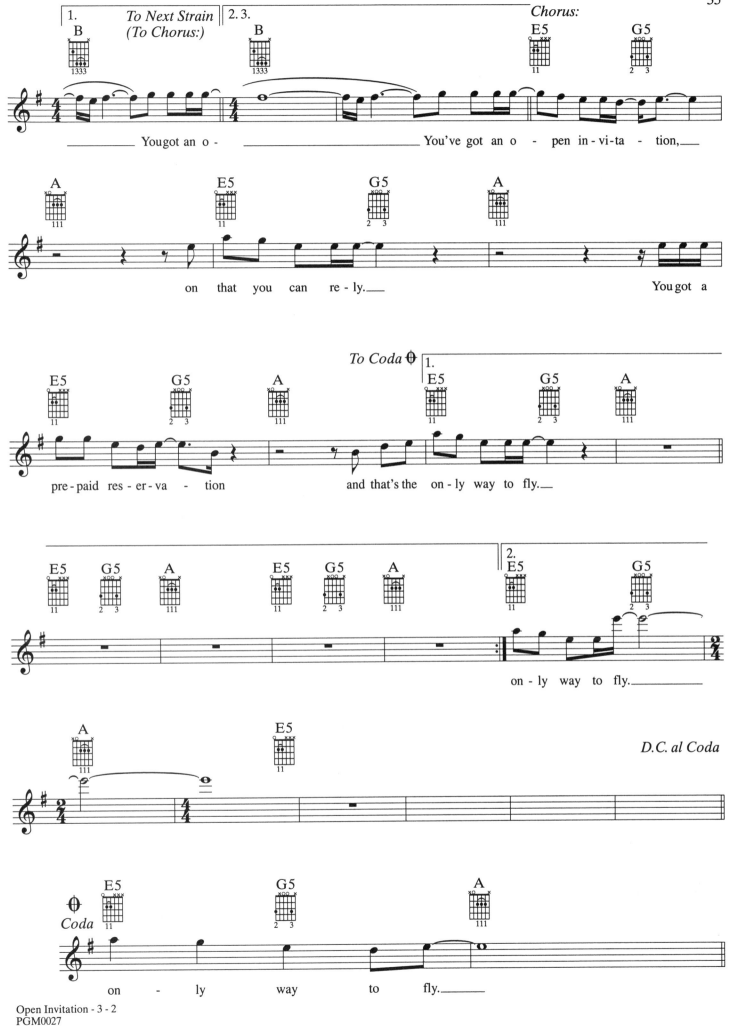

36

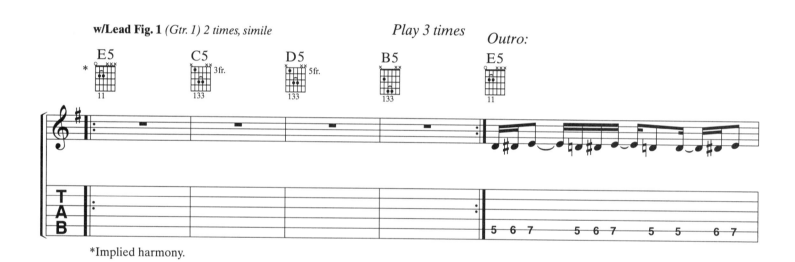

*Implied harmony.

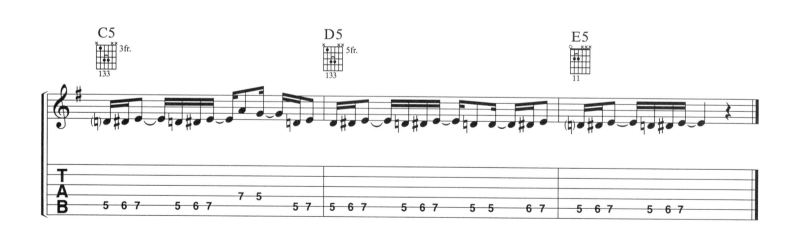

OYE COMO VA

Words and Music by
TITO PUENTE

© 1963, 1970, 1971 EMI FULL KEEL MUSIC
Copyrights Renewed
All Rights Reserved

38

Interlude:

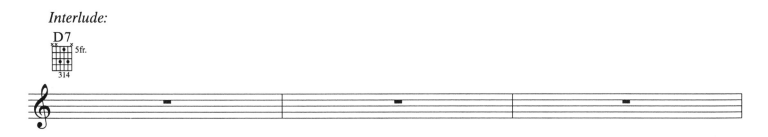

Guitar Solo: *Repeat as needed*   *Outro:*

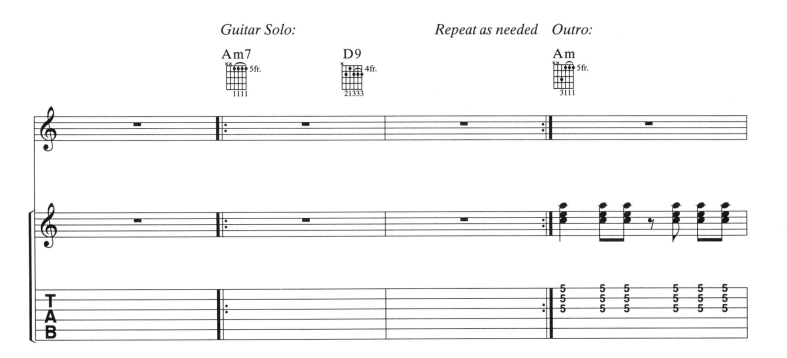

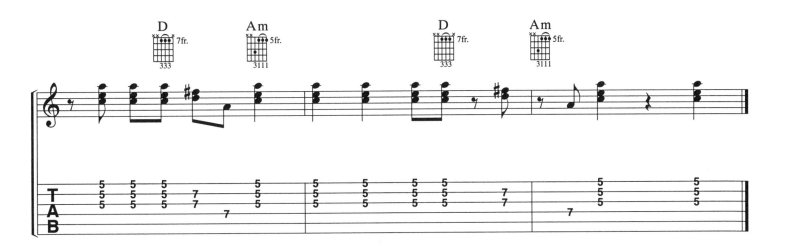

Oye Como Va - 3 - 3
PGM0027

PUT YOUR LIGHTS ON

Words and Music by
ERIK SCHRODY

Slowly ♩ = 72
Chorus:

Hey now, all you sin-ners, put your lights on, put your lights on.

Hey now, all you lov-ers, put your lights on put your lights on.

Hey now, all you kill-ers, put your lights on,
Hey now, all you sin-ners, put your lights on,

put your lights on. Hey now, all you chil-dren, leave your lights on,
put your lights on. Hey now, all you chil-dren, leave your lights on,

Put Your Lights On - 3 - 1
PGM0027

© 1999 IRISH INTELLECT and T-BOY MUSIC LLC
All Rights Administered by T-BOY MUSIC LLC
All Rights Reserved   Used by Permission

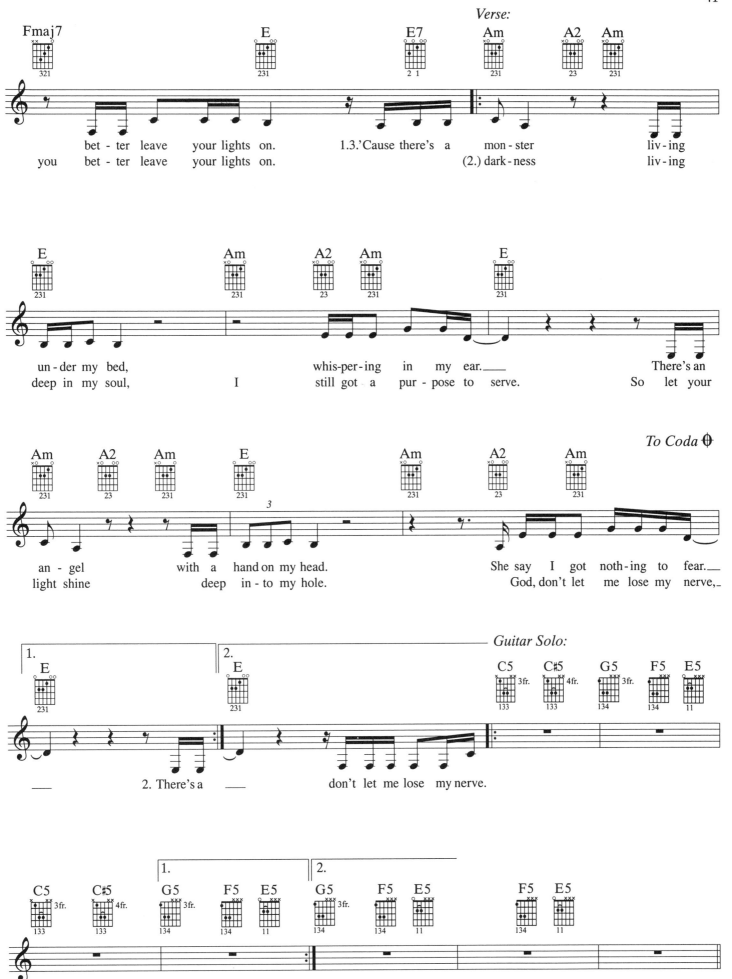

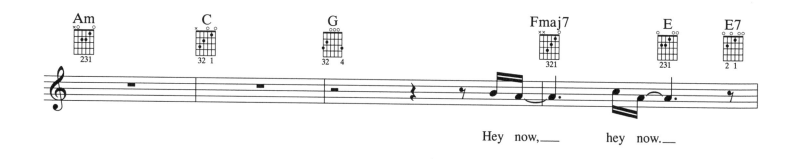

Hey now,___ hey now.___

D.S. % al Coda

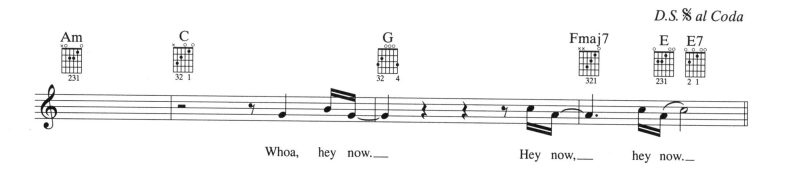

Whoa, hey now.___ Hey now,___ hey now.___

Outro:

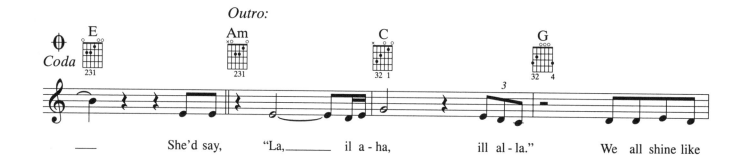

Coda

___ She'd say, "La,___ il a - ha, ill al - la." We all shine like

stars.___ La,___ ill a - ha, ill al - la. We all shine like

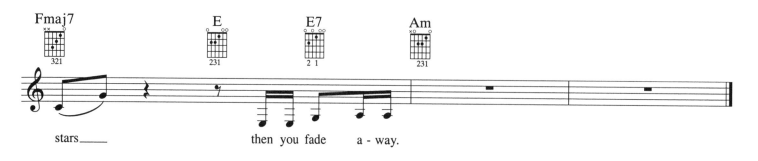

stars___ then you fade a - way.

SMOOTH

Lyrics by ROB THOMAS
Music by ITAAL SHUR and ROB THOMAS

Smooth - 3 - 1
PGM0027

© 1999 WARNER-TAMERLANE PUBLISHING CORP.,
ITAAL SHUR MUSIC, EMI BLACKWOOD MUSIC INC. and BIDNIS, INC. (BMI)
All Rights for ITAAL SHUR MUSIC Administered by
WARNER-TAMERLANE PUBLISHING CORP.
All Rights Reserved

44

Smooth - 3 - 2
PGM0027

48

So, here's the layout of all the notes in the Chromatic Scale up to the 15th fret, with the accidentals expressed as sharps. This diagram is here for easy reference; I mean, it's not like you need to concern yourself with memorizing all these notes!

I'd like to show the multiple locations of *one more note:* the high open E. Play all 4 positions of this note (circled below) and listen to the **tonal quality** of each. As you proceed up the neck, moving from the 1st to the 4th string, each successive E note sounds thicker, warmer and bassier, while the open 1st string E note sounds downright brash and tinny, yet they are all unison notes. Something to do with physics. I dunno.

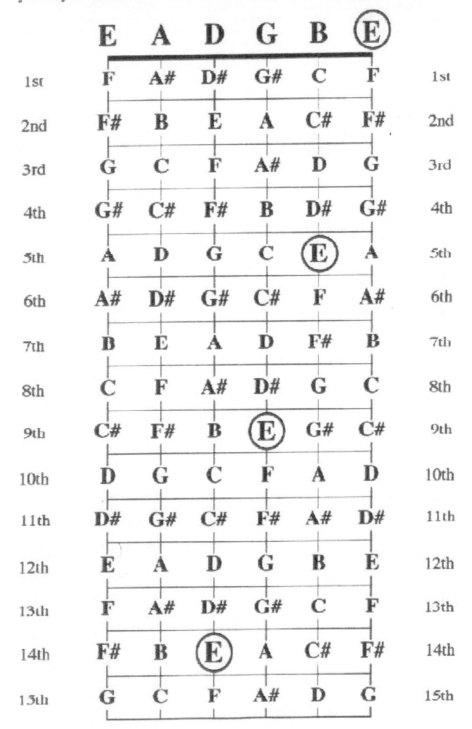

	E	A	D	G	B	E	
1st	F	A#	D#	G#	C	F	1st
2nd	F#	B	E	A	C#	F#	2nd
3rd	G	C	F	A#	D	G	3rd
4th	G#	C#	F#	B	D#	G#	4th
5th	A	D	G	C	E	A	5th
6th	A#	D#	G#	C#	F	A#	6th
7th	B	E	A	D	F#	B	7th
8th	C	F	A#	D#	G	C	8th
9th	C#	F#	B	E	G#	C#	9th
10th	D	G	C	F	A	D	10th
11th	D#	G#	C#	F#	A#	D#	11th
12th	E	A	D	G	B	E	12th
13th	F	A#	D#	G#	C	F	13th
14th	F#	B	E	A	C#	F#	14th
15th	G	C	F	A#	D	G	15th

45

Smooth - 3 - 3
PGM0027

SAMBA PA TI

Words and Music by
CARLOS SANTANA

Samba pa Ti - 2 - 1
PGM0027

© 1970 Careers-BMG Music Publishing, Inc.
All Rights Reserved   Used by Permission

SOUL SACRIFICE

Words and Music by
C. SANTANA, G. ROLIE,
M. MALONE and D. BROWN

Moderately fast ♩ = 172

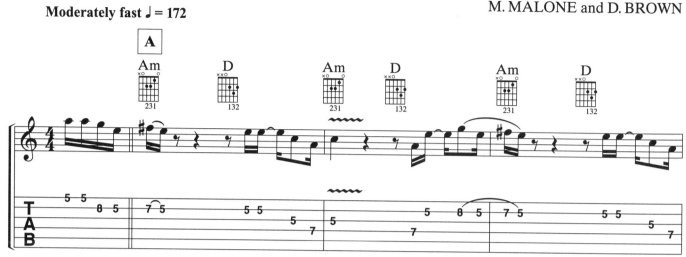

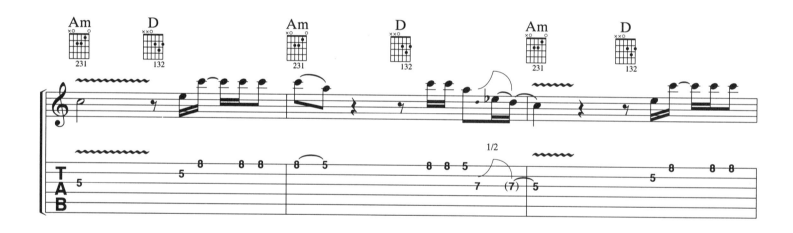

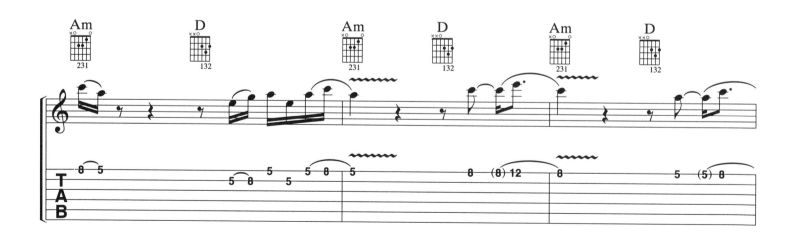

Soul Sacrifice - 5 - 1
PGM0027

© 1970 Careers-BMG Music Publishing, Inc.
All Rights Reserved   Used by Permission

50

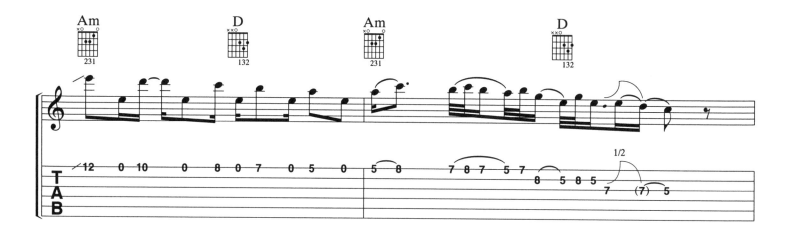

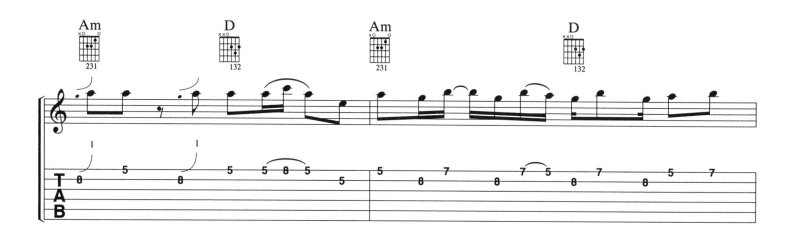

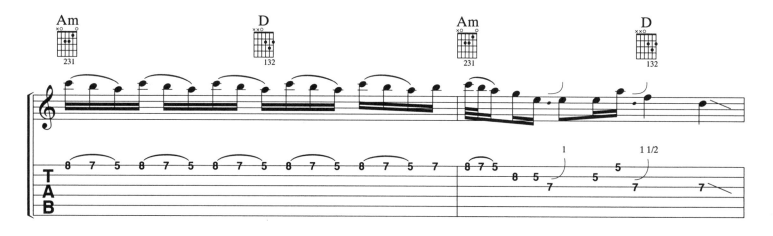

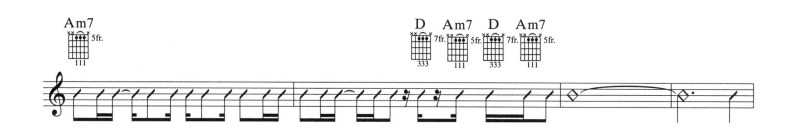

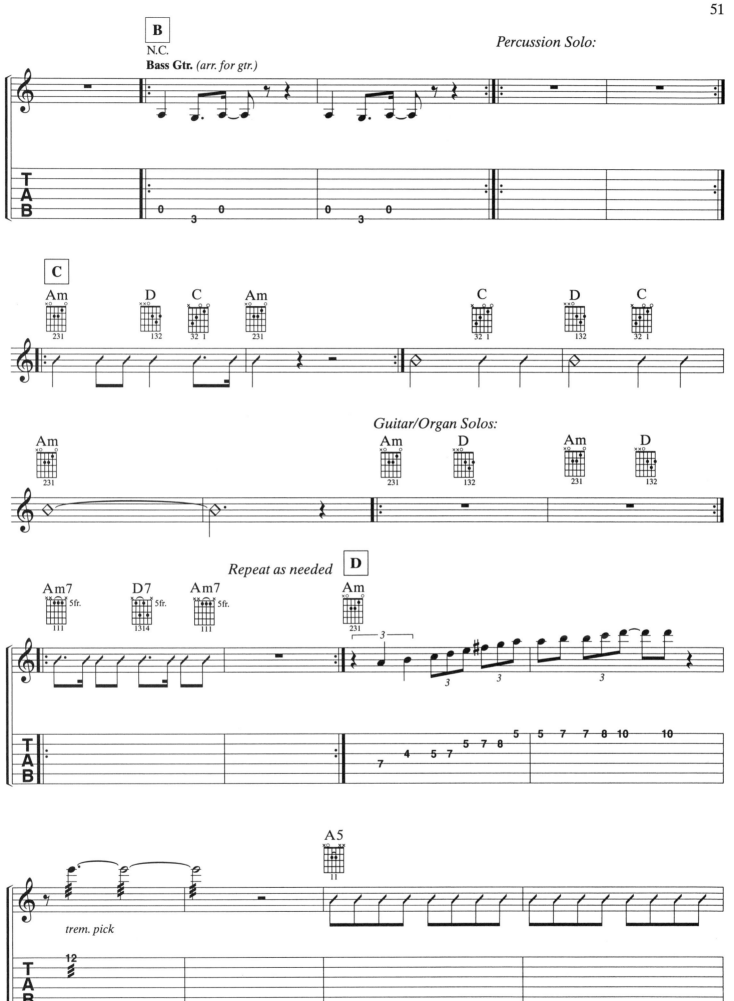

52

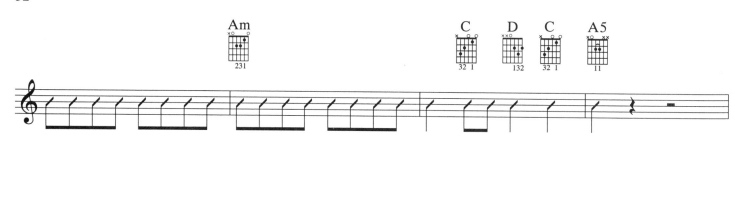

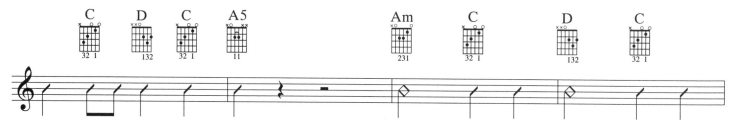

Outro:

Soul Sacrifice - 5 - 5
PGM0027

WISHING IT WAS

Words and Music by
EAGLE-EYE CHERRY, JOHN KING,
MICHAEL SIMPSON and MARK NISHITA

Slowly ♩ = 84
Verses 1 & 2:

1. Beau - ty and grace is what touch-es me most. Good times can put me in fear. I
feel - ing won't last 'cause I can - not sur - vive. I tell you I've been here be - fore. I'm

al - ways feel safe when things are bad.__ So I can - not let you come near. It
mov - ing so fast, it's a mat - ter of time. One of us walks out that door.

seems that I thrive in the dark side of things. I al - ways feel a - live when the death bell rings.

Chorus:

Now you come__ and you bring out the tears in me. Pain nev - er makes me cry__ but

© 1999 Universal - MCA Music Publishing, A Division of Universal Studios, Inc.,
Dust Brothers Music, Universal - MCA Music Ltd. and Diesel 2 Publishing & Management AB
All Rights for Dust Brothers Music and Universal - MCA Music Ltd.
Administered by Universal - MCA Music Publishing, A Division of Universal Studios, Inc.
All Rights for Diesel 2 Publishing & Management AB Administered by
Warner-Tamerlane Publishing Corp.
All Rights Reserved

hap-pi-ness does._ It's so strange to watch_ your life_ walk by_ and wish-ing it was._ Wish-ing it

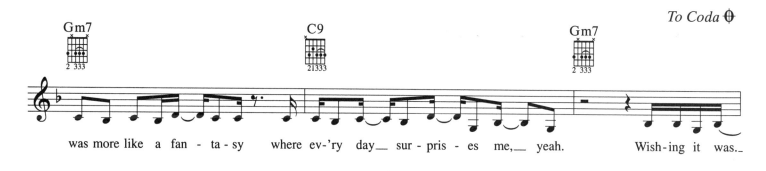

To Coda ⊕

was more like a fan - ta - sy where ev-'ry day_ sur-pris - es me,_ yeah. Wish-ing it was._

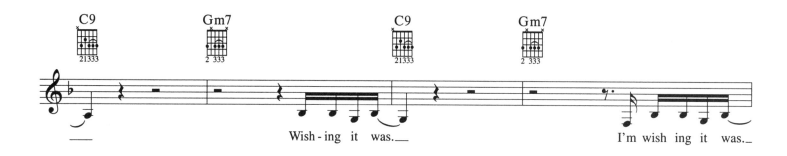

_ Wish - ing it was._ I'm wish ing it was._

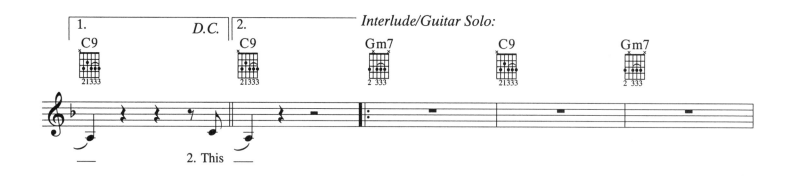

1. *D.C.* 2. *Interlude/Guitar Solo:*

2. This _

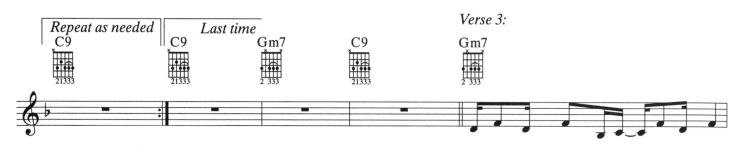

Repeat as needed *Last time* *Verse 3:*

Give this some thought, I'm sure_ you will know

STORMY

Words and Music by
BUDDY BUIE and J.R. COBB

Moderately ♩ = 114
Verse:

1. You are the sun - hine, ba - by,   when - ev - er you
2.3. Yes - ter - day's love was a - live;   the warm sum -

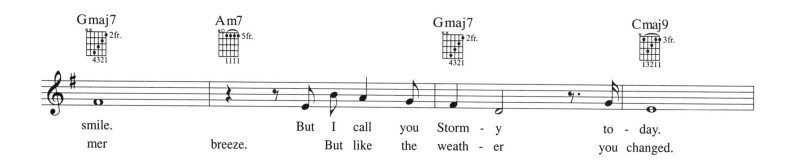

smile.   But I call you Storm - y to - day.
mer   breeze.   But like the weath - er you changed.

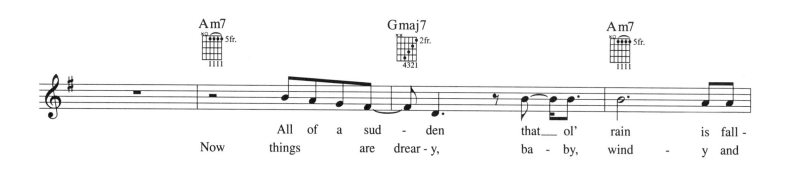

All of a sud - den   that ol' rain is fall -
Now things are drear - y,   ba - by, wind - y and

in' down.   And my world is cloud - y and gray;
cold.   And I stand a - lone in the rain

Stormy - 2 - 1
PGM0027

© 1968 Low-Sal Inc. (Renewed)
All Rights Reserved   Used by Permission

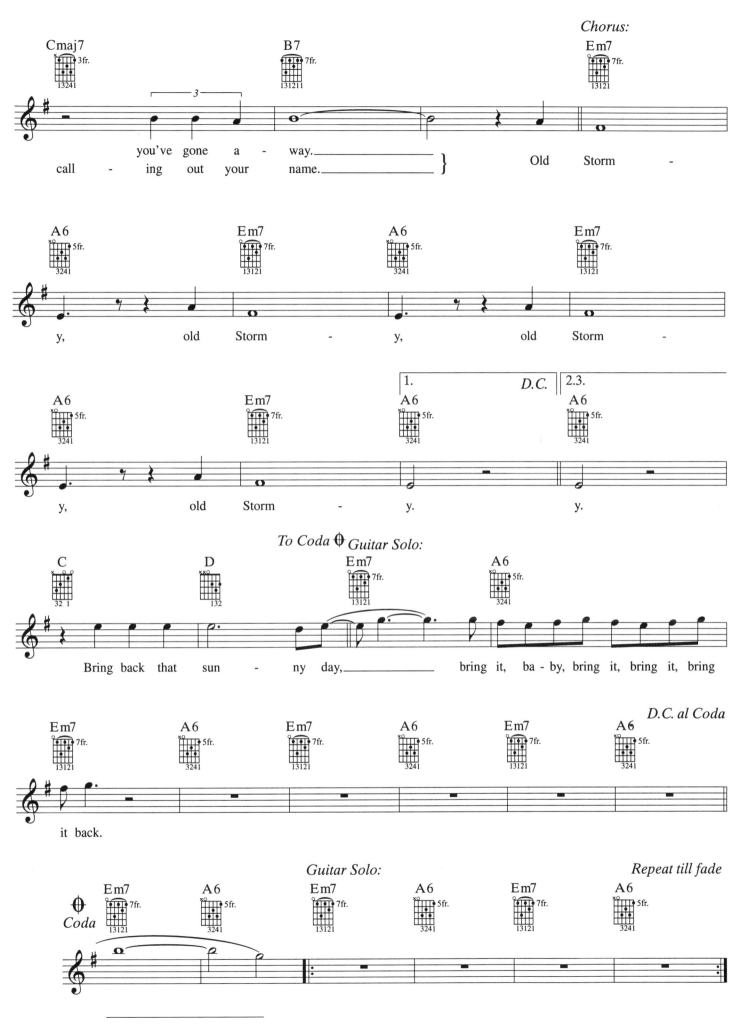

TRANSCENDANCE

Words and Music by
CARLOS SANTANA

© 1978 LIGHT MUSIC (BMI)
All Rights Reserved

WINNING

Words and Music by
RUSS BALLARD

Moderately ♩ = 84

Verse:

1. One day___ I was on the ground_ when I need-ed a hand_ and it could-n't be found._ I was
(2.4.) had a dream but it turned to dust and what I thought was love_ that must have been lust. I was
3. *See additional lyrics*

so far down that I could-n't get up. You know and one day I was one of life's los-er's,
liv-ing in style when the walls fell in. When I played my hand I looked like a jok-er.

e-ven my friends_ were my ac-cus-ers. And in my head, lost be-fore_ I'd be gun.
Turn a-round,___ fate must have woke her 'cause

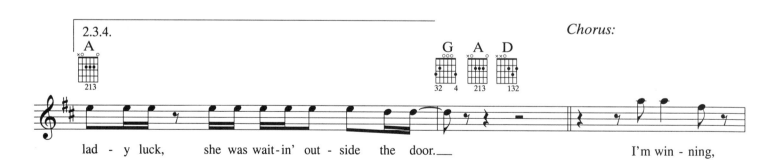

Chorus:

lad-y luck, she was wait-in' out-side the door.___ I'm win-ning,

© 1977, 1981 Island Music Ltd., London, England
All Rights Reserved for the U.S.A. and Canada by EMI Music Publishing
All Rights Reserved

I'm win - ning, I'm win - ning, I'm win - ning, I'm win - ning__ and I

don't in - tend__ on los - in' a - gain.__

To Coda 🔴 1. G A D *D.C.*

2. G A D *D.C. al Coda*

4. I

Guitar Solo:

🔴 *Coda* G A D E C#m

Play 3 times and fade

E C#m F#m B

Verse 3:
Too bad it belonged to me.
It was the wrong time
And I meant to be.
It took a long time
And I knew for now.
I can see the day
That I breath for.
Friends agree there's a need.
(To Chorus:)

(DA LE) YALEO

Words and Music by
S. MUTELA, H. BASTIEN, C. POLLONI
and CARLOS SANTANA

© 1999 SIXTE QUINT MUSIC PUBLISHING (Adm. by BUG MUSIC),
HONEY B. PUBLISHING (SACEM) and STELLABELLA MUSIC (BMI)
All Rights Reserved

le - o,_____ Ya - le - o._____

Ti-ka n'gai wa__ yo sim-ba n'gai wa__ yo ya ya. Ti-ka n'gai wa__ yo,

To Coda ⊕

Verse 3:

sim-ba n'gai wa__ yo ya ya.

Si tu pu-die-ras, de-cir-me a mi,

yo no lo cre-o lo que pa-sa a-qui. E-lla es mi-a y me da su a-mor. Es-toy com-ple-to y soy fe-liz. A-

D.S. 𝄋 al Coda

ho-ra ten-go ni-nos que di-cen Ya-le - o,___ Ya-le-o, Ya-

Solos: *Repeat ad lib.*

⊕
Coda

64